Original title:
The Shovel Shuffle

Copyright © 2024 Creative Arts Management OÜ
All rights reserved.

Author: Olivia Sterling
ISBN HARDBACK: 978-9916-94-196-6
ISBN PAPERBACK: 978-9916-94-197-3

Whispers of the Earth

In the garden, worms dance cheer,
With a jig and a twist, oh how they cheer!
Beneath the surface, they dig and dive,
While we just watch, feeling alive.

Every scoop brings laughter bright,
As dirt piles up, a comical sight!
With every chuckle, the soil unveils,
Secrets of laughter, in giddy trails.

Boogie in the Backyard

Under the sky, the trowel spins,
A groove erupts as the digging begins!
Grass and mulch, they join in fun,
With every shovelful, the party's begun!

Swing those hips, let the dirt fly wide,
As the flowers sway, joining the ride.
Churning the earth with a crazy beat,
In our backyard disco, there's no retreat!

Soil's Secret Sonata

Deep in the ground, a melody plays,
A symphony of soil, in quirky ways.
Each shovelful brings notes, so spry,
In this concert of dirt, we laugh and cry.

The radishes hum, the carrots croon,
While rain dances down, a sunny tune.
With every turn, the rhythm grows,
As we dance on this stage where the funny flow.

Shifting Through Shadows

As twilight falls, the shadows grow long,
We dig and we laugh, such a silly throng.
With a flick and a flop, the spade takes flight,
Our antics in twilight, oh what a sight!

Unearthing giggles in the fading light,
The garden a stage, our jester's delight.
From the depths of the earth, laughter erupts,
In the moon's glow, our joy disrupts!

Groundwork of Dreams

In a garden where shadows play,
A tool rests, ready for the fray.
With each dig, bright hopes arise,
Transforming earth to sunny skies.

The worms waltz in their newfound space,
As I dance with dirt, a carefree grace.
Oh, the laughter in each clod,
Creating beauty from the flawed.

Patterns in the Gravel

Walking on stones, I start to skip,
Each step a chance for a perfect trip.
Patterns form beneath my feet,
A rhythmic dance, oh what a treat!

I trip and tumble, back to the ground,
The gravel giggles, oh what a sound!
Stone by stone, I weave my tale,
Rough and ready, I shall not fail.

Dialogue with the Depths

I chat with clay as it's pulled high,
Whispering secrets, oh my, oh my!
The earth responds with a gentle sigh,
Together we laugh as the seasons fly.

With a chuckle, the spade digs in,
Uncovering treasures buried within.
Mirthful echoes fill the air,
In this playful, rich affair.

Leaps Over Layers

Jumping over dirt, feeling spry,
Each leap brings laughter as I fly.
Layers of laughter, soil and fun,
Beneath the sun, our games are spun.

With every shovelful, joy unfolds,
Tales of the ground and adventures bold.
In the mess of life, I find my way,
Playing in dirt, come what may.

Layers of Life

In the garden, we dig and play,
Finding treasures as we sway.
A worm wriggles, wearing a frown,
While we're busy turning the ground.

Seeds are planted, a dance of hope,
But we trip on roots, oh, how we grope!
Each shovelful leads to a story,
Of veggies, bugs, and squirrel's glory.

With every scoop, the laughter grows,
A mud pie here, a garden hose.
Who knew dirt could be such fun?
Under the sun, we've just begun!

So here's to the layers, all mixed and swirled,
In this messy, happy, garden world.

Digging for Whispers

With our spades we start to slide,
Uncovering secrets that nature hides.
A squirrel chats, a bird takes wing,
We laugh and wonder what they'll sing.

Each scoop reveals a tale untold,
Of timid roots that nations hold.
Digging deeper, we hear the ground,
Whispers of laughter, soft and profound.

A trowel here, a shovel there,
We're archaeologists of fresh air.
What's that? A button, a toy, a shoe?
Our digging tales would fill a zoo!

So come, my friend, let's dig some more,
With laughter echoing evermore.

Silt and Soliloquy

In the mud, lost in thought,
Life's little quirks are quickly caught.
We babble on, the soil's our stage,
With every clump, we flip the page.

Silt squishes beneath our feet,
Who knew dirt could be so sweet?
As we riff in the muck, ideas collide,
A concert of thoughts, our muddy pride.

With a rake and a grin, we sculpt the way,
Creating sculptures of clay and spray.
A masterpiece born from toil and fun,
We laugh as the work is never done!

So take a shovel, and join the quest,
Finding humor in dirt is the best.

Beneath the Surface

Beneath the surface, oh, what a view,
With every scoop, our friendship grew.
A dance of dirt, we twist and turn,
While sharing secrets, our hearts all yearn.

I found a crocus, blooming bright,
And giggled at the worms' delight.
They wriggle and squirm, in their own parade,
We'll tell their stories as we invade.

Let's unearth memories, one by one,
Of jolly digs and the joy we spun.
In our castle of mud, we reign supreme,
With laughter flowing, we chase the dream.

So grab a trowel, come take a dive,
In dirt and laughter, we come alive!

The Dance of the Displaced

In the yard where grass does sway,
A shovel and a spade at play,
They wiggle, jiggle, twist and turn,
While the neighbors stop and learn.

With every scoop, the dirt does fly,
Watch out for clouds up in the sky!
The dog joins in, a muddy mess,
While birds around them try to guess.

One shimmies left, the other right,
Poking holes—oh, what a sight!
Back and forth, they trade their roles,
Digging ditches, finding holes.

Laughter echoes, a raucous tune,
As sunlight fades, beneath the moon.
The earthworms cheer from below,
"Dance, oh tools, put on a show!"

Groundswell Melodies

From the shed, they rise and glide,
Brooms and forks, all side by side.
They kick up leaves, a swirling spree,
In the garden, oh what glee!

A hoe does twirl like it's a star,
While a rake sings loud, "I've come so far!"
Together they hum a cheerful sound,
Making music from the ground.

Spades crack jokes as they dig a hole,
Telling tales of garden goal.
With every scoop, a hearty laugh,
In this chore, they find their path.

Beneath the sky, with tracks they chart,
Digging deep with joyous heart.
Through soil soft and gravel tough,
They create art—this life's enough!

Rhythm of the Rake

A rake does dance with all its might,
Throwing leaves in the warm sunlight.
It sways and shakes with quite a flair,
While laughter echoes through the air.

Gathering scraps, it spins around,
Turning chaos into sound.
The garden's stage, a merry scene,
As it twirls like a dancing queen.

Each leap and bounce, a joyous quake,
With crowded grass, it starts to shake.
The compost bin has joined the fun,
As nature's harmony is spun.

In this ballet of dirt and green,
A funny sight, quite the routine.
With every stroke, a comic cheer,
As for the yard, they persevere!

The Earth's Chorus

The shovel sings, a baritone tone,
While trowels tap, the seeds are sown.
A melody bright, like sunny rays,
They work together in joyful plays.

Spoons and forks join in delight,
Twirling around, oh what a sight!
Planting dreams in rows so neat,
With every stomp, they find their beat.

The hoe hums low, a bassy drum,
While pruners strum their garden strum.
The earth rejoices, a rhythmic cheer,
Moving with laughter, spreading good cheer!

Under the sun, what a fine throng,
These garden tools can't get it wrong.
With every jingle, dance, and scoop,
They form a joyful, earthen troop!

The Dance of the Digger

In the garden, a spade takes the stage,
Wiggling wildly, it's all the rage.
With a twist and a twirl, it digs in deep,
Unearthing laughs, and secrets to keep.

Around the patches, the shovel prances,
Twirling soil, while the weed dancer glances.
Tickling roots, with a tap and a twist,
It's a party on earth, you can't resist!

Bouncing back and forth, the handle sways,
Making dirt jump in curious ways.
As if the clumps are caught in a groove,
The garden comes alive, in this silly move.

So join the fun, grab your own tool,
Let's dig together, we'll make it cool.
With laughter echoing through the plot,
When it comes to dancing, we can't be caught!

Rhythm of the Roots

Under the moon, the trowel starts the beat,
Digging and diving, what a treat!
Beneath the grass, the roots listen close,
To the funny rhythm, they giggle, engrossed.

Chop and pop, the ground breaks away,
In this earthy ballet, we love to play.
Worms join in, with their wriggly groove,
Each shake of the spade makes the garden move.

Laughter erupts with each clump of dirt,
As the plants sway in their leafy skirt.
With a flick of the wrist, the chaos unfolds,
In this rhythmic dance, our story is told.

When the stars shine bright, the night turns gold,
We dig up memories, and laughter unfolds.
Join the roots in this wacky delight,
In the rhythm of the garden, we'll take flight!

Labyrinth of Lines

A shuffle of spades marks the ground,
As we twirl and giggle, laughter's found.
Each line we create, a winding jest,
In this tangled dance, we're truly blessed.

Through muddy paths, we weave and sway,
Chasing our shadows, in joyful play.
Each scoop is a beat, each step a rhyme,
In our garden maze, we escape time.

The sun peeks in, with a curious glance,
Watching diggers take a silly stance.
We spin and we whirl, with every shove,
In this crazy plot, we dance with love.

The edges we trace with our spades held tight,
Create a maze that's a pure delight.
With giggles aplenty and roots in sync,
We're lost in the joy of dirt and drink!

Cadence of the Clod

In the dirt, we find a funky beat,
With each little clod under our feet.
A tap on the ground, and a bounce in the air,
It's a clumsily choreographed affair.

With a flick and a toss, the clods take flight,
A cheeky little dance in the moon's soft light.
The garden erupts in a giggly cheer,
As we shimmy and shake, with no hint of fear.

Chasing the sunlight, we leap and sway,
While the soil holds secrets, hidden away.
Each clump a partner, in this merry whirl,
As we dip and slide, what a silly twirl!

So grab your shovel, and join the fun,
In this dance of dirt, we're never done.
With laughter echoing through the clod and sod,
We'll shuffle forever, against all odds!

Pulse in the Pasture

In the field, a dance begins,
With a tool made for grins.
Digging holes and tossing dirt,
While the cows watch, unperturbed.

Frogs leap high, they join the fun,
As we dig 'til the day is done.
The rhythm of shovels clinks and clanks,
A symphony of muddy pranks.

Bunnies hop, they quite approve,
To the beat, we always groove.
With every scoop and silly slide,
Together, we laugh, and take it in stride.

So if you're feeling low and glum,
Grab a spade, let's have some fun!
A pulse in the pasture, wild and free,
Is how we mark our jubilee!

Motion in the Muck

In the muck where sneakers slip,
We gather for a joyful trip.
Clumsy moves, we twist and sway,
A comedic ballet in the clay.

Feet stuck fast, we laugh and snort,
As we dig up mud, a real sport.
Every shovel full, a choreographed act,
In this gunky world, it's a fact!

Pigeons coo, they watch the show,
As we tumble, in mud we flow.
A splash here, a squish right there,
Who knew that mud could be so rare?

With each round of our flinging spree,
We find joy in our muddy jubilee.
So let's groove and make a mess,
In motion, we find pure happiness!

Steps of the Excavator

We roll and slide, we twist and spin,
With shovels raised, let the fun begin!
Each step forward, a chance to play,
In our diggers, we feel okay.

Tired hands but eager grins,
As we clear the earth, it's where the fun begins.
Ladies and gents, a dance complete,
We groove to the rhythm of our muddy feet.

Giggling children, laughter loud,
We ex-cavate a joyful crowd.
With each scoop and playful jest,
In these steps, we feel our best!

Our motion's rhythmic, a jolly scene,
Digging with flair, we reign supreme.
Echoes of laughter rising high,
In the steps of joy, we reach for the sky!

The Earth Dancer's Journey

Underneath the sky so wide,
With shovels, we take pride.
Every inch, a story told,
As we dance with the earth, bold.

A twirl here, a scoop right there,
Digging deep without a care.
We glisten like stars, in the muddy dew,
The earth's embrace, wondrous and new.

With a chuckle and a wink, we glide,
Our shovels like partners, side by side.
Each toss of dirt, a laughter spree,
As we sway with nature, wild and free.

Our journey's not just toil or trade,
But a dance of joy we've made.
Emerging from this joyful spree,
The earth dancer's heart, forever free!

Beneath the Boughs.

Beneath the boughs, I take my stance,
With shovel raised, I start to dance.
The earth is soft, it begs to play,
I dig and giggle, lost in sway.

The sun above, a jolly friend,
As my eager hands begin to blend.
I strike a pose, a mighty knight,
In a battle with the dirt, what a sight!

With every scoop, I find a treasure,
A plastic toy, oh what a pleasure!
The squirrels watch with curious eyes,
As I twirl and leap, to my surprise.

At last I'm done, the hole is deep,
I take a breath, it's time for sleep.
But in my dreams, I hear the sounds,
Of dancing shovels beneath the grounds.

Digging Dreams

I grab my shovel, feeling bold,
Digging dreams of shimmered gold.
With every scoop, the stories grow,
Of buried secrets down below.

A worm pops up, gives me a wink,
As I imagine treasures in a blink.
Each pile of dirt becomes a tale,
Of pirate ships and phantom sail.

I laugh and toss the clumps around,
Making castles from the ground.
As dirt flies up, I strike a pose,
With soil-caked hands, I steal the show!

The laughter echoes through the trees,
You'd think I'm dancing with the bees.
Oh, digging dreams are quite the treat,
With every scoop, life is sweet!

Earth's Embrace

In Earth's embrace, I join the fun,
With my old shovel, I weigh a ton.
I hack and hoot with joy so loud,
To stir the soil, it's what I vowed.

The garden gnomes look on in awe,
As I dig deep, their smiles I draw.
A hop, a skip, and then a jump,
I'm dancing high, oh what a thump!

A rabbit peeks from grassy veil,
While I embark on this silly trail.
In dirt I find a sticky shoe,
A treasure trove of things I strew.

At day's end, the sun dips low,
I pack my tools, it's time to go.
But dirt in my hair, oh what a sight,
I leave with laughter, joy tonight.

Rhythm of the Dirt

With every beat, my shovel glides,
In a rhythm where mischief hides.
The dirt is soft, the sun is bright,
As I dance and dig with all my might.

A rock I find, it's round and slick,
I give it a toss, it lands with a flick.
The earth replies with a giggly sound,
As I shuffle and twirl around.

My friend the mole peeks from the ground,
He hums along with a silly sound.
We boast together, no need to compete,
In this merry dance, we can't be beat!

At last I stand, my work complete,
With muddy shoes and a dance-like feat.
So here I go, with joy abound,
In rhythm with the dirt, I'm glory-bound!

Rhythm of the Ridges

In a garden, we stomp and slide,
With every scoop, we take great pride.
A clump of earth, a flick of dirt,
We laugh and grunt with every spurt.

The wheelbarrow's wheels squeak and squeal,
As we dig and pile, it's quite the deal.
With every turn, a dance we do,
Ah, the joy when the soil flies too!

Neighbors peek, with a grin so wide,
Watching our antics, full of pride.
We gather sticks, we gather stones,
Creating chaos, while teaching bones.

So come and join our merry crew,
With a wave of spades and a shovel or two.
We'll turn this chore into a game,
With laughter echoing, fun is our aim.

Flow of the Furrow

We take the tools and get to work,
With shovels gleaming, not a quirk.
A little dance, a tip, a twirl,
As we dig holes and watch dirt swirl.

The soil's our stage, we dance so bright,
Furrows and ridges in the morning light.
With every shove, we sing a tune,
A farmer's chorus that makes us swoon.

The neighbor's cat joins our lively spree,
Leaping high, as happy as can be.
We toss the dirt, we spill some more,
Turning up soil like never before!

With laughter loud and spirits high,
We'll look back to see the clouds fly by.
Each scoop a giggle, each furrow a cheer,
Our garden dance is the best of the year.

Dance of the Digging Hands

A force of nature, hands at play,
With trowels swinging all the day.
We heave and hoe, each motion spry,
Digging so fast, we might just fly!

A little slip, a playful fall,
Covered in dirt, we're having a ball.
We high-five shovels and join the spree,
Hand in hand, it's pure jubilee.

The sun is bright, the shadows dance,
While worms wiggle, they take a chance.
To join our party of merry hands,
Laughing and digging in these fine lands.

So if you're down for a happy quest,
Join our crew, you'll be impressed.
With each dug hole, our spirits rise,
In a world of laughter, under clear skies.

Sway of the Spade

With spades in hand, we take a leap,
Into the soil, our laughs run deep.
A little wiggle, a little jig,
Watch us dig, then twist and zig!

The dirt flies up, a nearby bee,
Buzzes around, curious as can be.
We swing our spades like they're our friends,
In this wild dance, the fun never ends.

We toss the clumps in glorious view,
While giggles echo, all bright and new.
A muddy mess, but smiles so wide,
In this joyful toil, we take great pride.

So gather round, and join the spree,
With shovels swinging, oh so free.
We'll dig and dance until we drop,
With every rhythm, our laughter won't stop!

Shifting Soil Symphony

In a garden bright and glad,
A gardener's dance, oh what a fad!
With a spade that sings a tune,
Digging deep beneath the moon.

The earth spins round in clumps of cheer,
Each scoop of dirt, a giggle near.
With every turn, a jolly jig,
Unearthing treasures, oh so big!

Seeds fly like confetti in the air,
Laughter sprouts, a joyful flair.
When the wheelbarrow's wheels go clack,
It's a party as we haul it back!

So grab your tools, let's have some fun,
With every toss, we're on the run.
In dirt there's magic, pure and sweet,
Join the ballet of the muddy feet!

Tilling the Silence

In a quiet yard with soil so deep,
We dance and twirl, our laughter leaps.
Each turn of the fork, a playful prance,
Stirring up joy in this garden dance.

The shovels gleam under the sun,
As we dig and laugh, oh this is fun!
Roots peek out with a cheeky smile,
Greeting us with their earthy style.

Worms wiggle in a wiggly row,
Spreading giggles as we go.
A clod flies loose, a soft "whoops" sound,
Laughter rings out all around!

So come, my friends, the soil awaits,
Let's till our worries—leave the fates!
In this garden, we lose all strife,
With every handful, we reclaim life.

Echoes in the Earth

With shovels held like magic wands,
We whisper secrets to the sands.
Each echo of our toil and cheer,
Resonates, the fun is clear.

Kicking clods, we hear the sound,
Of laughter and dirt tumbling around.
Digging down, we find a prize,
As giggles echo to the skies.

The rhythm of our heels so light,
Turns work to frolic, pure delight.
Every scoop brings forth a grin,
Earthy treasures buried within.

So join the song, it's your turn too,
To dance with dirt and chuckle, woo!
In this earthbound ball, we're all the same,
United in laughter, in this fun game!

Underground Euphoria

Down below where critters bide,
We dig with glee, and never hide.
Each burrow deep, a tale unfolds,
In a patch of earth, our fun beholds.

With shimmering shovels and a clunky scoop,
We're crafting chaos in this muddy troop.
Oh, look! A rock that's shaped like a shoe,
Splashes of dirt paint us all anew!

Tiny roots reach up for air,
They poke and prod, a friendly dare.
As we uproot more, our giggles soar,
What's hidden below? Oh, let's explore!

Let laughter rise with every thrust,
In this earth's ballet, we do trust.
With each cheeky shovelful we take,
We find pure joy, for laughter's sake!

Digging Dreams

In the yard with glee I roam,
My trusty tool becomes my home.
I dig for treasures, shiny and bright,
But find only worms, what a sight!

Each scoop a laugh, each turn a jest,
Who knew dirt would be my quest?
I talk to moles, they give me shade,
Together we prank, and plans are made.

With every pile, my hopes take flight,
I wave to neighbors who giggle with fright.
What lies below? I can't quite tell,
But I'm on a mission, digging quite well!

So join me in this soil-filled game,
For finding something is my aim.
With laughter echoing, I keep it light,
In my backyard fantasy, what a delight!

Earth's Rhythm

With a wiggle and a flop, I take my stance,
Each scoop a step in a quirky dance.
Blades cut through earth, a strange ballet,
While ants form lines and cheer me on my way.

The ground shakes softly with every swing,
As squishy things dodge—a lively fling.
A worm twirls up, joins in the fun,
Together we jig until the day is done.

I swear I hear a melody sweet,
And chuckling critters keep the beat.
With dirt on my shoes and a grin so wide,
This digging fest is a rollicking ride!

So let's shimmy in the soil today,
For in the dirt, who needs ballet?
Embrace the chaos, the muddy turns,
In this earthy rhythm, my spirit burns!

Unburied Secrets

What lies beneath this patch of green?
Stashes of wonders, yet unseen?
With my shovel in hand, I take the plunge,
Unearth old toys and a donut sponge.

The dog barks loud at every find,
An old shoe sole, what a bind!
A rusted key, but to what? Who knows?
Each whiff of dirt, my nose it blows!

I'm a pirate on this treasure hunt,
With voices in my head to confront.
"Dig deeper!" they call, "You'll be a star!"
But all I see is a smelly jar.

Yet laughter spills from my every dig,
For memories shine like a childhood jig.
With each unearthing, a silly cheer,
What treasures hide in my backyard here?

A Dance with Dirt

With feet that slide and hands that fling,
In muddy mess, I find my zing.
A twirl here, a scoop there,
Who knew dirt could bring such flair?

I've got the moves; they're wild and free,
The earth my stage, come dance with me!
With every cast and every spin,
I laugh at the mess—oh, let's begin!

Sunshine glimmers on a grubby face,
A jig with worms, oh what a place!
Silly little critters join the show,
In this messy ballet, they steal the glow.

So grab a shovel, don't be shy,
Let's turn this soil, reach for the sky.
In this frantic dance of dirt and fun,
We'll giggle and jiggle till day is done!

Burdens Unearthed

In the garden where weeds do grow,
I dug up treasures, quite the show.
A rubber chicken and a sock,
What madness lies in soil and rock!

With every scoop, a laugh escapes,
Finding odd things, like funny shapes.
A pair of glasses, a toy train,
What else will pop up from the grain?

A shovel game, it's never dull,
Each new find, a joyful lull.
A buried hat, it fits just right,
Oh, the wonders in the night!

Digging deeper with glee and cheer,
Unearthing stories, year by year.
In each mound, a scene unfolds,
Burdens become laughter, bright as gold.

When Shadows Dig Deep

Beneath the surface where shadows play,
   Odd things waiting for light of day.
  I tossed the dirt with all my might,
    A circus elephant, what a sight!

A shovel swings with a clumsy arc,
Out pops a cat with a quirky spark.
Each little find makes me chuckle,
  In this comedy, I start to shuffle.

The ground reveals its playful side,
 A treasure map to nowhere wide.
Peeking out from a muddy hole,
 An old record of rock and roll!

What tales do you hold in your embrace,
  Oh, universe beneath my space?
When shadows dig, all becomes clear,
  In laughter's wake, I persevere.

The Rhythm of Ridges

With every thrust, a nascent groove,
The rhythm of digging, watch me move.
A wiggly worm begins to dance,
As I uncover a long-lost prance.

The hillocks sway, the valleys chuckle,
In this landscape, I start to buckle.
Each scoop whispers a secret tune,
Digging up cosmos, the sun and moon.

The beat goes on as I lift and toss,
A shiny button, a story glossed.
From dirt and grit, a giddy spree,
Every jangle is sheer glee!

Jumping rhythm, I stumble, I sway,
To each odd treasure that comes my way.
The dance of dirt wraps me tight,
A joyous jig in morning light.

Moving Mounds

In a pile of earth, the fun begins,
As I chuck the clay, let laughter spin.
A rubber duck, bright yellow and neat,
Buried treasures, oh what a feat!

Mounds of dirt, a time machine,
Discoveries hide, oh how obscene!
Out pops a sandwich, oh what a treat,
Digging can lead to surprises sweet!

The shoveling's sweet, a vigorous sport,
Each mound shifted, a comical sort.
With every toss, a giggle, a roar,
What lies beneath, forever more!

As I move the earth with zest and flair,
A magic realm beneath my care.
From wacky finds to memories grand,
In this playful game, I take a stand.

Unearthing Echoes

In the garden, a spade so bright,
I keep digging deep, what a sight!
Each clump of dirt, a hidden prize,
A worm's surprise, oh, how it flies!

With every scoop, the laughter grows,
Such antics found beneath the rows.
A shoe that's lost, a toy from years,
Digging up my childhood fears!

Neighbors watch with curious grins,
What will I find? Let the fun begin!
A trowel dance, in dirt we twirl,
Each twist and turn, a wacky whirl!

In this dig, who knows what's there?
A treasure chest or just thin air?
Yet in this soil, the joy's the gold,
As stories of my shoveling unfold!

Dance of the Dig

In the backyard, we gather round,
With spades in hand, no fun is drowned.
A rhythm starts with every thrust,
We kick up dirt, it's a must!

Shuffle to the left, then to the right,
A shuffle here feels just so right.
Each scoop brings giggles, what a show,
As worms wiggle with the flow!

Turn to my friends, with arms in play,
We make the soil dance away.
With every lunge, we burst with glee,
Hey — did I just find a key?

The sun beaming down on our parade,
In this dirt jam, we're unafraid.
With laughter loud, the day we fill,
Digging and dancing, what a thrill!

Buried Beats

In the dirt, the rhythm starts,
As we dig, we share our hearts.
A beat kicks in with each small scoop,
While grooving with a brand new group!

Left foot in, then right foot out,
What treasures hide, we laugh and shout!
A rock, a coin — what will we land?
In this treasure hunt, we make a band!

With every shovel, the tunes we weave,
What stories deep does soil conceive?
A raucous cheer for every find,
In this dance, we leave behind!

Oh the giggles, they never cease,
As dirt reveals our joys and peace.
So join the beat, together we play,
Digging up fun in a crazy way!

Grains of Motion

Dirt clouds swirl, it's quite the race,
With shovels held at frantic pace.
Grains of laughter fill the air,
What will we find? We do not care!

Digging here, a digger's dream,
Each scoop reveals a funny theme.
A garden shoe, a doll we see,
Our backyard's historic mystery!

Shake it, rattle, let's give a cheer,
With every hit, the fun draws near.
A treasure hunt, a silly quest,
Who knew dirt could be this blessed?

Join the merry band, my friends,
With every shovelful, laughter blends.
We dance through earth, in joyful motion,
Buried beats create our commotion!

Hands in the Soil

In the garden, I take a stance,
My hands dig deep for a little dance.
Wiggling worms join in the fun,
As I shuffle dirt under the sun.

Trowel twirling, oh what a sight,
Soil flies up, a cloud of delight.
Potatoes peek out, peeking so sly,
I tip my hat as they wave goodbye.

Bugs start to boogie, oh what a treat,
With every shovel, I hop on my feet.
The radishes giggle, and carrots say hey,
It's a jazzy jig in the dirt every day.

Hands in soil, the joy is vast,
With every bucket, I'm having a blast.
So here's to the fun, the dirt, and the toil,
Every garden dance, a treasure of soil.

Choreography of the Earth

Out in the garden with a grand flair,
I shuffle around as I breathe fresh air.
Seeds in my pocket, dancing to grow,
I lead the way with a warm, sprightly flow.

A little hoe hop, a twist to the left,
I'm a dancing gardener, truly bereft.
Of all formal training, but who needs that?
When the daisies and I just I must chit-chat!

Digging and gabbing, oh what a pair,
The sun on my back, with light, I repair.
With laughter and joy ringing clear all around,
The earth joins my jig, in rhythm we found.

Cantaloupes bouncing, a jolly good time,
Rhythm of roots, nature's own mime.
So join in my frolic, it's never too late,
This earth-waltzing way is simply first-rate!

Motion Beneath the Surface

Beneath the earth, a party's begun,
Wiggly life dancing, oh so much fun!
With spades scooping soil, oh what a scene,
The ground's got a beat, and it's wild and keen!

The trowel taps out a rhythm so sweet,
A jiggle and jangle, we shuffle our feet.
The roots join the chorus, a chatty affair,
As I move through the dirt with dance-like flair.

Up pops a radish, it winks with a grin,
"Let's boogie together, come join in the spin!"
With each little push, a laugh and a cheer,
The soil's great ballet brings everyone near.

Underneath all the chaos, there's joy to be found,
So kick up your heels, let's dance on the ground.
With every shovel's fling, new life comes to play,
Beneath the surface, there's fun every day!

The Art of Excavation

With a clatter and clang, I start my big show,
As I dig through the earth for treasure below.
Each scoop of dirt, a musical score,
In this grand exhibition, who knows what's in store?

Old toys and faded seeds come out in a whirl,
When I lift up the shovel, it starts to twirl.
The clods are my dancers, each one with a flair,
As I shuffle along without a single care.

The earth does a jig, and I can't help but grin,
With every new scoop, I just dive right in.
A shovel's not tool, it's a wand of delight,
Turning dirt into smiles, what a magical sight!

So here's to the laughter we find in our toil,
The art of excavation, love of the soil.
Next time you dig, don't forget to have fun,
And join in the dance under the warm sun!

The Syncopation of Silt

In the garden, I prance and play,
With a scoop and a twist, I dance all day.
Dirt flies high in a clumsy arc,
Who knew my feet could leave a mark?

Laughter echoes with each little thud,
As I fumble through clumps of mud.
Nature's rhythm, a messy jam,
Every shake, a 'whoops'—oh, ma'am!

I dig for treasures, but find only clay,
This silt-filled shuffle just made my day.
With flips and flops, I lose my grace,
Yet every slide brings a smile to my face!

So here's to the dirt and the silly strides,
In this earth-filled dance, pure joy resides.
With every tremble, I sway and sway,
Join the fun—it's a muddy ballet!

Earthbound Footfalls

With boots of brown, I stomp around,
Every step a giggle, oh what a sound!
The soil shifts with my jolly gait,
Dance like a chicken? No, I can't wait!

Wobbling out on this shaky ground,
Twirling in circles, I spin round and round.
Knees to the dirt, I fall with a thud,
I'm just here creating my masterpiece of mud!

Each little leap is a comical sight,
As I juggle soil in the soft twilight.
My neighbors peer out with curious eyes,
Wondering who's lost to the earth and the skies!

Oh footfalls bound in this earthy fun,
With giggles and snorts, I'm never done.
In my clay-studded shoes, I proudly strut,
With every new shuffle, I leave my cut!

Rhapsody of the Relic

Found a relic beneath the tan,
An old rusty tool—I'm a digging man!
With a twist and a turn, it's harder than gold,
But it's a perfect prop for this story to unfold!

As I shimmy and shake with this treasure in hand,
The garden becomes a stage, oh how grand!
With each silly beat, I paint the ground,
In a symphony of laughter, joy is found!

My costume's dirt, my audience ferns,
As history giggles, this clay pot churns.
I trade my shovel for laughter and fun,
Every clink and clang? A new pun begun!

So let's spread glee with each dig and drag,
In the earth where memories gather and brag.
With whimsical rhythms, let's dance through the day,
In this rhapsody of relics, we'll laugh and sway!

Tilling Time

Time to till, oh what a chore,
But with a giggle, I'll make it much more!
My trusty fork, a dance partner true,
Together we jiggle, just me and my crew!

With every little poke, I jump and shout,
My raucous laughter echoes all about.
We uproot weeds that think they can stay,
But with a hop, I send them away!

Each clod that shatters, each twist of the spade,
Turns work into play—a fabulous parade!
The worms join the fun in a wriggly line,
As I create chaos—oh life is divine!

So bring on the dirt, bring on the grime,
I'll sway with the veggies, it's tilling time!
With every small misstep, I hoot and I holler,
In this garden of giggles, let joy be the scholar!

Dance of the Earthbound

In muddy boots we take our stand,
The rhythm shifts across the land.
With every scoop, we form a beat,
And laugh as clay gets on our feet.

Our partners twirl with buckets bright,
As shovels clash, what a delight!
We jig and jive with heaps of dirt,
A ballet in the garden's skirt.

The garden gnome joins in the fun,
Waving at the setting sun.
We sway to nature's quirky song,
As laughter echoes all night long.

When morning comes, the dance won't cease,
We'll dig for joy, a small piece.
With every laugh, we find our groove,
In a world where all can move.

Ground Game Gala

A shovel's jab, a quick embrace,
We leap across this softened space.
With every swing, we hit the ground,
In this gala where fun is found.

Together now we strike a pose,
Dodging dirt and garden knows.
A mound of soil - what a prize,
We giggle at the silly size.

The neighbors peek with feigned disdain,
'What's that racket?' they complain.
But in our hearts, we're feeling grand,
At this gala, hand in hand.

We strike a final pose at dusk,
Just dirt and jokes, no need for fuss.
With tired limbs, we bid goodbye,
Oh what a scene under the sky!

Artist of the Acre

With shovel strokes, a canvas wide,
We dig and dance with utmost pride.
A masterpiece of earth and cheer,
The laughter draws our friends so near.

Brushstrokes of dirt become our art,
Each pile a laughter-filled part.
With every heave, we sculpt the scene,
A quirky show, quite unforeseen.

We mix the soil like paintbrushes,
Creating chaos, oh how it crushes!
But as the sun fades in the west,
We marvel at our muddied quest.

An ode to nature, wide and free,
An artist's heart is all we need.
Tomorrow calls, but tonight we smile,
For in this dirt, fun walks a mile.

Wading Through the Wilderness

With shovels poised, we brave the muck,
In this wild land, we're truly stuck.
Each squelching step brings giggles near,
As nature's mess becomes our cheer.

We wade through weeds and piles of clay,
Trading our tools, we shout 'Hooray!'
Every toss and turn brings bliss,
Who knew that dirt could feel like this?

A raucous crew in garden's grip,
We laugh until our voices slip.
Like playful children on the run,
In our wild world, we've just begun.

So here's to mud and nature's jest,
We'll dance and dig, forget the rest.
With every shovelful, joy we gain,
In wilderness, we'll entertain.

Caverns of Hidden Tales

In caverns deep where echoes play,
Old tales are found, come out and stay.
The dirt is loose, the laughter flies,
As hidden gems bring bright surprise.

With every scoop, a noise erupts,
A clumsy lunge, the ground disrupts.
A sparkling stone, or maybe muck,
Yet with each find, we just can't luck.

Digging deep in boots so old,
The humor here is worth its gold.
We tumble, trip, and then we scream,
For what's a find without a dream?

So join the fun, the dirt and grin,
For every quest, we shed our skin.
These caverns sing with tales so grand,
Get ready now, let's make a stand!

The Unearthing Song

With shovel clinks and joyful shouts,
We dance around, forget our doubts.
A treasure here or maybe there,
Just watch your step, or paint the air!

As we dig down, the soil flies,
Each clod reveals where laughter lies.
We find old bones or something cute,
Can't stop the giggles—who knew it'd hoot?

The sun is bright, our hats askew,
In this strange game, it's all brand new.
A vintage shoe? A rusty fork?
The weirdest finds are quite the cork.

So sing along, oh heart so bold,
In dirt we trust, in fun we hold.
Each scoop a note in our sweet song,
Come, dig with us; you can't go wrong!

Depths of Discovery

Into the ground, we gleefully dive,
With shovels gripped, we're so alive.
Each spade turns earth, a sight to see,
Unearthing joy and mystery.

What lies beneath? The question flares,
Each clunky thud, igniting pairs.
A rolling stone or maybe dirt?
We laugh so hard, we start to spurt!

In layers deep, our dreams unfold,
A pocket watch, or a figure bold?
Or is it junk? Who really knows?
In every find, our laughter grows!

So let's not stop till dusk appears,
With every scoop, we shed our fears.
In depth we seek, through muck we trot,
In discovery, we find our plot!

Echoing in the Earth

Oh hear that sound? A joyful thump,
In caverns low, we take a jump.
The shovel sings, in dirt it grins,
In echoes here, our laughter spins.

With trembling hands, we dig for gold,
Yet find a shoe that's worn and old.
In histories lost, we place a bet,
Our funny finds, we won't forget.

The deeper we go, the more absurd,
Each scoop reveals what seems unheard.
From rattled bones to marbles bright,
The earth has secrets, what a sight!

With every clank, our spirits rise,
The echoing fun, a grand surprise.
So join the crew, let's laugh and play,
In the earth below, we'll find our way!

Treading on Time

With feet that dance on muddy ground,
The rhythmic plop is quite the sound.
As I stumble left and trip to the right,
Laughing away from morning to night.

Tools in hand, oh what a sight,
Wobbling like a wobbly kite.
Time's a jokester, playing this prank,
With every shift, there's laughter to crank.

Digging holes like a grinning fool,
Finding treasures that none could school.
A garden plot that's shaped like a pie,
Oh, what fun, as the worms all sigh.

With each small shovel, a giggle grows,
Unlikely paths where no one knows.
As I churn and churn, a comic ballet,
In this wild dance, I'll forever stay.

Cadence of the Ground

In a flurry of feet, the earth does sway,
Each squeaky step leads me astray.
With a rhythm that's strange, I twirl and bend,
Planting seeds of laughter, forgot to tend.

The melody plays, my hips start to groove,
As I dig and plunge, I find my move.
Bouncing back, I stumble wide,
Mother Nature's disco, let's enjoy the ride!

A funky choreography in the dirt,
With laughter ringing, no one gets hurt.
Clods of soil become my stage,
The crowd of crows squawk, "What a strange age!"

With the sun as a spotlight, I dance around,
Turning every patch into a playground.
It's not just work, but a playful jest,
In the rhythm of soil, I find my quest.

Shifting Landscapes

Cranky clumps that cling to shoes,
Oh, these paths, do they amuse?
With every shove, I make a mess,
Creating chaos, oh what distress!

Like a game of tag, the earth will play,
With unexpected turns that lead you astray.
A hop, a skip, mud launches high,
Splat! My friends just laugh and sigh.

The landscape changes with each silly step,
A cartwheel here leads to a misstep.
As I frolic through the squishy land,
Life is a jest when a shovel's in hand.

In this arena of laughter and glee,
Even the soil seems happy to be.
With each little shove of that trusty spade,
I find new paths where memories are made.

Unearthly Moves

With a chuckle and giggle, I make my way,
Each shove of the tool leads me to play.
Floating on air, or perhaps on muck,
My feet feel lighter with each little cluck.

Dance steps in dirt, I'm losing my aim,
Gardening? No! It's a whimsical game.
A waltz with worms, the carrots take flight,
Me tripping and slipping, oh what a sight!

The soil beneath starts to hum my tune,
As I dance with the daisies, under the moon.
Planting with flair, I swirl and twirl,
While my garden plots giggle and whirl.

With each little poke at the earth's soft belly,
I craft a tableau that's bright and jelly.
This earthen jig, a laugh so divine,
In the dance of the garden, I'm feeling fine.

The Soil's Serenade

In the garden, we dig with glee,
Worms dance joyously, can you see?
The spade makes sounds, a rhythmic beat,
While dirt flies up, oh what a treat!

We laugh as we trip on the way,
Throwing mud like kids at play.
The flower pots sway, all in tune,
As we revel under the bright moon!

With every scoop, a chuckle rings,
The joy of toil, oh, what it brings!
Hands may be muddy, shirts may snag,
But it's all part of this garden brag!

So gather around, join the fun,
In this earthy dance, we've just begun!
With giggles and wiggles, we take our stand,
As the soil sings, oh isn't it grand?

Choreographed in Clay

With a twirl and a kick, we dig away,
Planting laughter in the light of day.
Our tools do a jig, how odd, how neat,
As we dig to the rhythm, oh, feel the beat!

The shovel glides, a fancy step,
Muddy footprints, a tailor-made rep.
Our laughter echoes, a sweet refrain,
In the frolic of toil, who feels the strain?

Each scooping motion brings a clap,
A comedy act or a silly map.
Our hearts grow light, and dirt flies high,
As we choreograph beneath the sky!

So let's dance with shovels, all in a row,
In a clay-filled ballet, just watch us go!
With a wink and a grin, we take our chance,
And giggle our way through this spirited dance!

Underfoot Harmonies

The soil beneath begins to hum,
As we stomp and shuffle, here we come!
With each footfall, a squishy sound,
The rhythm of gardening, joy abound!

In the muck, our shoes embrace,
Creating tunes in this mucky place.
Up sprouts a plant, just like a joke,
In this muddy choir, we all evoke!

With a wink, a nudge, we go off-track,
Fallen seeds, let's bring them back!
To each other, we toss a jest,
In the wild concert, we feel so blessed!

So dance, dear friends, in dirt and glee,
With every misstep, our spirits free.
In this earthy ballet, we find delight,
As the soil sings through day and night!

The Seed's Waltz

A seed takes flight on a breeze so light,
As we sway and twirl, oh what a sight!
With every sprinkle, we make a wish,
In this garden stage, there's magic swish!

We waltz with weeds, a tangled embrace,
While giggles blend in this leafy space.
A hop and a skip, then down we go,
In this whirl of green, we find our flow!

Each scoop brings laughter, each seed a dream,
In this dance of dirt, we're a happy team.
With boots that squelch and hands in the air,
The fun multiplies with every share!

So let's keep spinning, oh come what may,
In this seed-filled ballet, let's laugh and play!
With each little sprout, another surprise,
In the rhythm of growth, joy never dies!

Echoes of the Earthbound

A tool in hand, I dig with glee,
The earth does giggle, just wait and see.
Worms and critters dance in delight,
While I swing and twist in the morning light.

Each scoop is filled with secrets untold,
A treasure of dirt, oh so bold.
With every clump, I can hear them cheer,
The earthbound creatures, they hold me dear.

So let's all rally, in this muddy mess,
We'll laugh and tumble, no need to stress.
For in this game of nature's art,
I'm but a jester with a joyful heart.

And as I caper on this patchy ground,
The universe giggles, what a funny sound!
With joy in each shovel-full's embrace,
I dance with the earth in this holy space.

Unveiling Nature's Notes

With a flick of the wrist, I make a mark,
Nature's symphony begins to spark.
Dirt flies high, like confetti in air,
I chuckle softly, does anyone care?

Each shovelful whispers secrets of old,
While squirrels gather, oh so bold.
They cheer me on, their tiny paws clapping,
With each little scoop, I'm happily mapping.

As daisies observe, they sway in time,
I'm the conductor of this joyful rhyme.
The orchestra plays, with roots and twigs,
It's a riot of laughter, the joy of digs!

So here I stand, my shovel in hand,
Creating a rhythm across the land.
Nature's notes echo, both wild and free,
In this comical dance, it's just dirt and me!

Steps Beneath the Stars

Kicking up dust under the moon's glow,
I shuffle and twirl, putting on a show.
The stars are grinning, what a sight,
As I dig and dance into the night.

Each step a giggle, each turn a cheer,
The ground beneath feels frolicsome here.
I'm a comet of chaos, a whirlwind of joy,
Chasing shadows, I'm nature's toy!

With the night's cool breeze playing the tune,
I dig in rhythm, under the moon.
Every scoop's a tickle, a funny delight,
In this enchanted moment, all feels right.

As laughter erupts from the cosmos wide,
I'm twinkling with glee, there's nowhere to hide.
Steps beneath stars are wild and grand,
A merry jaunt, hand in muddy hand!

Movement Under Moonlight

With shadows waltzing, I join the dance,
My shovel's my partner, oh what a chance!
Under the moonlight, we slip and slide,
The earth is my stage, where antics collide.

Each clang and clatter is laughter's decree,
From wriggling worms to a bumblebee.
They hum along, with joy in their flight,
While I frolic and dig in the still of night.

Every move I make is a jig of sorts,
A little dirt tango with critters and ports.
A whirl through the weeds, a laugh in the air,
Tonight's a comedy, a whimsical affair!

So round and round under glowing skies,
With friends made of dirt, oh how time flies!
In movement under moonlight, I feel alive,
As laughter and love in my heart thrive!

Movements in the Mud

In the garden I hop and I slide,
With each step, my shoes take a ride.
Wobbling and twisting, I lose my cool,
Oh, how I wish I could follow the rule!

The earth beneath me begins to squish,
Each shove and each stomp is a slippery wish.
Neighbors watch with a laugh and a cheer,
As I dance through the dirt without any fear!

Swells of the Subsurface

Burrows and dips, oh what a sight,
Every time I dig, I wiggle with fright.
The ground seems to giggle beneath my feet,
As I navigate chaos while searching for sweet!

One moment I'm sinking, the next I'm afloat,
My footing is tricky, I might be a goat.
Laughter erupts when I trip and I fall,
Footprints like puzzles, they baffle us all!

Tones of Tread

Marching along, with my boots full of glee,
Each stomp brings a sound that is silly to me.
The squelch and the plop, a melodic refrain,
As laughter erupts from each misstep again!

Up and down, around I must bound,
With the mud bringing music to my happy sound.
Jumping like frogs, we leap through the muck,
Oh, what a blast! We've got all the luck!

Transitions in the Terrain

Each patch of mud is a slippery tease,
Feet shifting like dancers, oh how they please!
With a tumble and twist, I roll like a ball,
Creating a scene that's amusing to all!

From gritty to glossy, the ground plays its tricks,
As I shimmy and shuffle through each dip and fix.
With friends all around, we share in the fun,
In this clubhouse of dirt, we can't help but run!

Echoes of the Earth

In the garden, I dig in delight,
Each toss of the dirt brings silly fright.
Worms wiggle and squirm in the soft, rich ground,
As laughter erupts with each clumsy sound.

A gopher peeks up, gives me a stare,
I wave to the critter, show I'm quite aware.
With shovels in hand, we dance 'round the plot,
Making a mess, but I care not a jot.

The earth gives a chuckle, an audience in play,
While mud splatters wildly, stalking my way.
In every quick dig, there's a twist and a turn,
Echoing giggles, my heart starts to burn.

Yet buried in laughter, a treasure awaits,
Old toys and coins, oh what fun this creates!
With each little find, I skip and I hop,
In this playful endeavor, I never will stop.

Shifting Soil Serenade

With a gleam in my eye, I grab hold of the spade,
A song of the soil begins to cascade.
Each scoop of the ground is a note in the air,
As I hum to the rhythm, without a care.

The neighbors all peek from their windows, they grin,
Watching my dance as I chuckle and spin.
The daisies join in, swaying side to side,
A natural chorus in this muddy slide.

I trip on a root, a most comical sight,
But the earth laughs along, sharing pure delight.
With dirt on my face and mud on my shoe,
I swing the old shovel, still breaking through!

And what do I uncover? A rubber duck bright,
Time-traveling treasure from my youth, what a sight!
Beneath layers of laughter, a whimsy unfolds,
Serenading the soil, where the magic beholds.

A Jolt of the Jaw

Digging down deep kicks up quite a show,
A dance of the dirt makes my worries all go.
As I shove with a grunt, a pebble takes flight,
Smacking my neighbor—oh, what a delight!

She shouts through the fence, 'That's quite a farewell!'
I grin and I wave, 'It's a mud pie to sell!'
In this wacky arena, where laughter connects,
I take on the soil with some funny side effects.

The shovel goes whoosh, like a tongue in a joke,
With each little fling, I feel quite the bloke.
A worm takes a bow, it wriggles with pride,
As I crack up the ground, feeling joy in the ride.

And under the rubble, a treasure does gleam,
A rubber band ball—it's a wacky dream!
So jolt with a laugh, and let worries drift,
For here in the dirt, life's the ultimate gift.

Secrets from the Spade

With a swipe of the blade, a secret's exposed,
A hidden old treasure, now quite decomposed.
What fun lies beneath this turbulent turf?
A patchwork of stories, a grinning old surf.

A trowel in tow, I'm the queen of the plot,
Each dig brings a mystery, treasures forgot.
The earth whispers clues, a chuckle it gives,
As I battle with roots that swirl like they live.

An ancient old spoon, with a tale to disclose,
Besides it, a shoe, in a half-finished pose.
I giggle and muse over stories long past,
And wonder if footprints tell legends that last.

So come join the quest, let's pry up some fun,
With secrets uncovered, the digging's begun.
In this whimsical garden, where laughter's displayed,
Every shovelful feasts on the joy we've portrayed.

Joy Beneath the Surface

In a garden so lush, I find my fate,
With a spade in my hand, it's never too late.
Digging for treasures, I strike gold,
My neighbor's old boots? Now that's something bold!

Worms are my audience, they wiggle and squirm,
As I dance with my shovel, I giggle and squirm.
Each scoop is a story, each mound a delight,
Who knew gardening brought such pure, silly flight?

Beneath the brown earth, secrets reside,
A rubber chicken found? Oh, what a wild ride!
With laughter I burrow, nothing to lose,
Every turn of the dirt, I just can't refuse!

So here's to the digging, the glee and the cheer,
With a wink and a grin, let's bring out the gear.
A world of odd wonders, beneath grass and vine,
In the joy of this shuffle, I happily shine!

Steps Among the Stones

With each little step, a thud and a clap,
I trip on a stone, then I fall in a lap.
Gravel's my foe, oh, the tales it could tell,
Of clumsy antics where giggles swell!

Sidewalks are stages for dancing so grand,
My feet all a-stutter, can't quite understand.
Each step is a puzzle, I giggle and sway,
Should I leap or just slide? Decisions, hooray!

The sun winks at me as I stumble about,
My dance with the stones, filled with laughter and doubt.
It's a wobbly tango, a quirky ballet,
Two left feet in motion, come join in the fray!

So who needs a floor when there's pebbles around?
I'll jive through the garden, a fool on the ground.
With mischief and joy, I'll keep to my tone,
Every step that I take is a step I own!

Routines of the Rural

A rooster crows early, the start of my day,
But my coffee spills over, oh, what a display!
I scurry and splatter, a sight quite absurd,
Who knew rural life came with such a blur?

Milking the cows is a dance by itself,
With a moo and a chuckle, and no need for stealth.
I skip and I stagger, my boots full of muck,
Bovine ballet? It's a real stroke of luck!

The pigs in their pens are my audience now,
They snort with approval, oh, take a bow!
Chasing the chickens, they flap and they flee,
"Get back here!" I shout, "You're not faster than me!"

So here's to the routine, the laughter it brings,
From dawn until dusk, oh, how my heart sings.
In the quirks of the country, I've surely found glee,
Where the mischief in chores makes life quite a spree!

Land's Hidden Lullaby

In fields so wide, where the tall grass waves,
Whispers of laughter float over the graves.
The earth has its secrets, I dig to unveil,
A spoon full of giggles and a bucket of tales!

As I twirl through the clovers, I stumble and sway,
Every patch has a story, in a comical way.
A tumble and roll, now look at me go,
Finding joy in the dirt, it's quite the show!

The crickets are chirping, a bard for the night,
While I lark with the daisies, what a funny sight.
With a flap of my hands and a skip in my heart,
This land plays the music, it's a world set apart!

Oh, let the moon shine on my ridiculous dance,
With laughter as my partner, I'm lost in the trance.
Beneath the soft starlight, my worries take flight,
In nature's good humor, everything feels right!

Composing in Clay

In the garden with glee, I take a stance,
Wielding my tool, it's a merry dance.
Every scoop a laugh, each turn a surprise,
I'm an artist of soil, with mud as my prize.

With a wiggle and shake, I create a mound,
Oh, look at the shapes that I've freshly found.
An arena of dirt for a critter parade,
Watch out, little ants, my plan's well laid.

The neighbors all chuckle, as I stomp about,
With a flick of my wrist, I send soil out.
Like a magician, I pull from the ground,
A masterpiece born, and laughter abound.

So next time you pry at that stubborn earth,
Remember it's fun, remember its worth.
A symphony in mud, of humor and toil,
Join in the banter, let joy soil!

Soil's Silent Motion

Under the sun, with my trusty spade,
Digging down deep, not a moment delayed.
With every light toss, my hat takes a flight,
just like my dreams, all soaring in sight.

The worms start to wiggle, they join in the show,
As I sing silly songs, and let my joy grow.
A dance with the dirt, it's the finest of plays,
A whimsical waltz through the garden's arrays.

Each clump is a chuckle, each toss a delight,
I giggle and snicker, from morning to night.
Messy and merry, this treasure I seek,
Funny finds in the mud, oh so unique!

So when life seems heavy, just give it a whirl,
Grab a shovel, my friend, and give it a twirl.
The soil will respond, with laughter in tune,
As we dance in the dirt 'neath the glow of the moon.

Terrain of the Treader

With a stomp and a boogie, I take on the ground,
This place is my playground, joy knows no bounds.
Scattered clods giggle as I make my way,
In this quirky escapade, I'm here for the play.

A slip, a slide, an unplanned ballet,
My feet will not listen, they're leading the way.
Like a dance floor of mud, it's a slippery sight,
Every twist and turn, a raucous delight.

Gazing in wonder, the critters all cheer,
As I trip to the left, then lurch to the rear.
With a hop and a skip, I'm the star of the scene,
A funny farm frolic, in my dirt-smeared jean.

So take up your shovel, come join in the fun,
In the silly mud games, we all shall run.
With laughter and cheer, as we shake up the land,
Treading the terrain, come on, take my hand!

The Plowman's Performance

Out with my shovel, I greet the day,
The earth starts to smile in a welcoming way.
With comedic finesse, I launch each new scoop,
A jester in dirt, in this playful troop.

The plants roll their eyes as I jump and I jive,
"Is that really a dance?" they seem to contrive.
But each little clod, each glittering sprout,
Joins in my antics, there's laughter throughout.

My hat takes a tumble, and I stagger with flair,
While I wiggle and waggle without any care.
Like a clown with a spade, I'm on a roll,
Transforming the garden into a comedy bowl.

So gather your gear and let's turn up the fun,
We'll make every furrow a carnival run.
As long as we chuckle and dance on this plot,
A plowman's performance will tie us in knot!

Whispers of the Ground

With a clatter and a clang, they go,
Digging deeper, faster, just for show.
Each scoop a giggle, a toss in the air,
Nature's secrets laid out, with flair.

Beneath the grass, curious things lie,
Lost socks, old toys, and maybe a pie.
They dig and they dance, a merry parade,
While rules of the garden begin to fade.

In the soil, stories from ages past,
A jumbled treasure, surprises amassed.
Neighbors peep out, and chuckles burst free,
As the crew of diggers giggle with glee.

Every tap, every thud, a rhythmic delight,
A comedy show, beneath day and night.
With each tiny triumph, a laugh takes flight,
In this digging escapade, everything feels right.

The Excavator's Waltz

Two friends with shovels begin the dance,
Twisting and turning, a whimsical chance.
They aim for a plot, yet dig so wrong,
Turning their chaos into a song.

With a scoop and a dip, they spin with glee,
Who knew a hole could bring such esprit?
They laugh at the dirt that flings every way,
Creating a mess that just begs to play.

In the muck, their boot prints chart a route,
A muddy canvas where dreams take root.
Oh, how the neighbors peek through the gate,
Wondering what kind of fun they create.

As they shuffle and sway, laughter fills the air,
What was once a task, now a comical affair.
With each hearty chuckle, the garden grows bright,
This merry escapade brings pure delight.

Path of the Gravedigger

With a wink and a nod, they plot their way,
A mischievous grin for the work and the play.
Pretending it's serious, digging so deep,
Yet laughter erupts as they trip and leap.

Each shovelful stirs up giggles so loud,
As they sculpt funny shapes, living their shroud.
A grave for a raspberry, an honor bestowed,
Yet their wild imagination, gleefully flowed.

An audience watches, some start to cheer,
For unexpected joy sprouts forth from their fear.
In this land of buried dreams and bright beams,
Laughter is gold, or so it seems.

With each playful toss, they dance in delight,
Creating a spectacle, a comic insight.
As day turns to dusk, the fun never ends,
These gravediggers prove they are true-time friends.

Beneath the Surface

They plunge down low with tools all around,
Unearthing treasures beneath the brown ground.
From silly old cans to photos of cats,
Each find leads to giggles, like quirky spats.

Underneath the shade of an old, creaky tree,
They discover lost items from days wild and free.
A shoe with a tale and a spoon with a twist,
In this world of mystery, nothing's amiss.

Shovels like dancers, they're rhythmically swayed,
Every slosh of the earth feels like a parade.
With laughter erupting, they ain't feeling shy,
Who knew the ground held such fun as they pry?

In their playful pursuit, joy blooms anew,
For every small find gives a laugh that will strew.
Beneath the surface, life bursts forth in cheer,
With each little treasure, the fun draws near.

Grounded Grooves

With a wobble and a jig, I take my stance,
Digging through the earth, I seize my chance.
The dirt flies high, like a dancing swirl,
I laugh at the chaos, watch the mounds unfurl.

Each scoop is a step, in this quirky dance,
Kicking up clods, oh, what a chance!
A shovel's embrace leads my feet astray,
I twirl and I spin, in the mud I play.

Neighbors peek out, they can't help but stare,
As I cha-cha with soil, without a care.
In my garden of mess, I'm the joyful king,
With every grain tossed, my heart starts to sing.

So join in the rhythm, let's uncork the glee,
In this funny venture, there's none but thee.
With each earthy scoop, we'll laugh till we drop,
In our grounded groove, let the good times pop!

Sweeping Through Shadows

In the twilight's glow, I grab my tool,
Casting long shadows, oh, isn't it cool?
With a sweep and a scoop, I'm a ghostly sight,
Dancing with shadows, oh what a night!

The clang of the metal, a comical sound,
I'm digging for laughter, it's all around.
As I plunge in the dirt, I start to find,
That silly old grin that's been left behind.

Like a raccoon in slippers, I shuffle about,
Turning up treasures, there's no room for doubt.
With a flip and a flap, I'm giddy with cheer,
In this shadowy realm, there's nothing to fear.

So when darkness falls, and giggles commence,
Grab your gear, take a chance, lose your sense!
For in the night's sweep, adventures await,
With giggles and grins, we can't hesitate!

Pulse of the Plow

With rhythm in hand, and dirt on my shoes,
I dance around mounds, in my joyful blues.
The pulse of the plow keeps me in tune,
As I jig through the fields, under the moon.

Each clod that I toss is a beat in my song,
With shovel as partner, I can't go wrong.
Dancing through furrows, raised high with delight,
Spinning and twirling, oh what a sight!

The neighbors all chuckle, they laugh at my show,
As I glide through the ground, moving to and fro.
A whimsical flurry, I make quite a scene,
While heartily grinning, like a playful queen.

So hit that sweet rhythm, let's shake up the earth!
In the pulse of the plow, we find joy and mirth.
Though dirt may be flying, and laughter will grow,
We'll dance through the night till the morn's early glow!

Melody of the Mound

In a garden so lush, where the laughter abounds,
I don my old boots, and I start my rounds.
With a flick of my wrist, and a grin on my face,
I'm composing a tune with this muddy embrace.

Each mound in the path sings a jolly refrain,
As I shuffle and scoop, like it's in my veins.
I tap on the soil, keep the rhythm alive,
With a chuckle and cheer, oh, this is the drive!

The moonlight is bright, casting shadows so wide,
Every clump that I toss brings a giggle inside.
Join me in this melody, don't be afraid,
In the harmonic dirt, friendships are made!

So let's dance in the soil, where laughter will bloom,
With the melody of mounds, we'll brighten the room.
Let's shovel together, with joy in our hearts,
This funny little waltz, where the fun never departs!

Milton Keynes UK
Ingram Content Group UK Ltd.
UKHW020043271124
451585UK00012B/1033